QUAKER OATS

OLD FASHIONED

CLASSIC RECIPES

pil
Publications
International, Ltd.

Favorite Brand Name Recipes at www.fbnr.com

Pictured on the front cover (clockwise from top left): Mu Shu Meatball Wraps *(page 40)*, Quaker's Best Oatmeal Cookies *(page 68)*, Spicy Oat-Crusted Chicken with Sunshine Salsa *(page 38)*, and Oatmeal Scotchies *(page 77)*.
Pictured on the back cover (top to bottom): Caramel-Nut Sticky Biscuits *(page 8)*, Dilled Salmon Cakes *(page 44)*, Fudgy Banana Oat Cake *(page 58)*, and Oatmeal Chipper Skillet Cookie *(page 66)*.

ISBN-13: 978-1-4127-2955-0
ISBN-10: 1-4127-2955-6

Manufactured in China.

8 7 6 5 4 3 2 1

Microwave Cooking: Microwave ovens vary in wattage. Use the cooking times as guidelines, and check for doneness before adding more time.

40

CONTENTS

12

50

Celebrating more than a century of classic family recipes

When you see the smiling man on the Quaker Oats package, you're likely to remember steaming bowls of oatmeal and fresh-from-the-oven oatmeal cookies—and with good reason. Since 1877, Quaker Oats has been America's favorite hot cereal and one of the most popular baking ingredients. In fact, in 1908 Quaker Oats introduced the very first package with a recipe printed on it—an oatmeal cookie.

The recipes on the package have changed over the years, but the great taste and wholesomeness of Quaker Oats have remained the same. Besides adding whole grains to recipes, versatile oats also have a delicious nutty flavor and chewy texture.

The recipes selected for this collection were developed in the Quaker Oatmeal Kitchen, a trusted source of recipes for many generations. Whether you've been cooking and baking for years, or are just beginning to explore the kitchen, you'll love this recipe collection. And for more great recipes, visit our website: www.quakeroatmeal.com

Know Your Oats

● Oatmeal is a whole-grain food. When oats are harvested, their inedible outer hull is mechanically removed, but the bran, endosperm, and germ of the whole oats remain intact. The oats are then steamed and roasted.

● Ounce per ounce, instant, quick, and old-fashioned oats are equally nutritious. The whole oat is rolled flat to become old-fashioned oats, or cut into smaller pieces and rolled thinner to make quick or instant oats.

Cooking and Baking with Oats

● You can use either Quick or Old Fashioned Quaker Oats when cooking or baking. Quick oats are simply cut smaller and rolled thinner to cook faster.

● Every time you bake, you can replace up to one-third of a recipe's flour with oat flour made from Quick or Old Fashioned Quaker Oats. Just whirl oatmeal in a blender to grind it into flour.

● Add ¾ cup oats per pound of ground beef or turkey when making meatloaf.

● Use oats in toppings for fruit crisps or crumbles.

● Quick or Old Fashioned Quaker Oats can be eaten uncooked. Enjoy oats added to salads, smoothies, sandwiches, and yogurt. For example, stir oats, diced fresh fruit and sliced almonds into low-fat yogurt, or sprinkle oats onto a peanut butter and jelly sandwich.

● Oats make a tasty, crispy coating for meat, chicken, or fish. Simply dip each serving in beaten egg whites, coat with oats, then bake in the oven.

● For a calcium boost, use fat-free (skim) milk instead of water when preparing hot oatmeal.

Where do the calories in a serving of oatmeal come from?

Nutrient	Grams per serving	Calories per gram	Calories per nutrient
Complex Carbohydrates	26	4	104
Simple Carbohydrates	1	4	4
Protein	5	4	20
Fat	2.5	9	23
Total Calories			151

Caramel-Nut Sticky Biscuits

Topping

⅔	cup packed brown sugar
¼	cup light corn syrup
¼	cup (½ stick) margarine, melted
½	teaspoon ground cinnamon
1	cup pecan halves

Biscuits

2	cups all-purpose flour
1	cup Quaker® Oats (quick or old fashioned, uncooked)
¼	cup granulated sugar
1	tablespoon baking powder
¾	teaspoon baking soda
½	teaspoon salt (optional)
½	teaspoon ground cinnamon
⅓	cup (5 tablespoons plus 1 teaspoon) margarine
1	cup buttermilk*

Sour milk can be substituted. Combine 1 tablespoon vinegar or lemon juice and enough milk to make 1 cup; let stand 5 minutes.

1. Heat oven to 425°F. Combine first four ingredients in small bowl; mix well. Spread onto bottom of 9-inch square baking pan. Sprinkle with pecans; set aside.

2. For biscuits, combine dry ingredients; mix well. Cut in margarine with pastry blender or 2 knives until crumbly. Stir in buttermilk, mixing just until dry ingredients are moistened. Knead gently on lightly floured surface 5 to 7 times; pat into 8-inch square. Cut into 16 (2-inch) square biscuits; place over topping in pan.

3. Bake 25 to 28 minutes or until light golden brown. Let stand 3 minutes; invert onto large platter. Serve warm.

Makes 16 servings

Nutrition Information (1 biscuit): *Calories 247 (calories from fat 105), total fat 12g, saturated fat 2g, cholesterol <1mg, sodium 250mg, carbohydrates 33g, dietary fiber 2g, protein 4g*

Oatmeal Carrot Cake Bread

  1   cup Quaker® Oats (quick or old fashioned, uncooked)
 ½   cup fat-free (skim) milk
  1   can (8 ounces) crushed pineapple in juice, undrained
  4   egg whites or 2 eggs, lightly beaten
 ¼   cup vegetable oil
  1   teaspoon vanilla
2½   cups all-purpose flour
  1   cup packed brown sugar
  1   tablespoon baking powder
 ½   teaspoon baking soda
 ½   teaspoon ground cinnamon
 ¼   teaspoon salt (optional)
1½   cups shredded carrots (about 3 medium)
 ½   cup raisins

1. Heat oven to 350°F. Lightly spray bottom only of 9×5-inch loaf pan with nonstick cooking spray or grease lightly.

2. Combine oats and milk in medium bowl; mix well. Let stand 10 minutes. Add pineapple (including juice), egg whites, oil and vanilla; mix well.

3. Combine flour, brown sugar, baking powder, baking soda, cinnamon and, if desired, salt in large bowl; mix well. Stir in carrots and raisins. Add oat mixture to dry ingredients all at once; stir just until dry ingredients are moistened. (Do not overmix.) Pour batter into pan.

4. Bake 60 to 75 minutes or until wooden pick inserted in center comes out clean and crust is golden brown. Cool in pan on wire rack 10 minutes. Remove from pan. Cool completely. Store tightly wrapped.

Makes 1 loaf

Nutrition Information (¹⁄₁₆ of recipe): *Calories 200 (calories from fat 35), total fat 4g, saturated fat <1g, cholesterol 0mg, sodium 140mg, carbohydrates 37g, dietary fiber 2g, protein 4g*

Apricot-Banana-Almond Bread

2½	cups all-purpose flour, plus flour for dusting pan
1	cup Quaker® Oats (quick or old fashioned, uncooked)
2	teaspoons baking powder
1	teaspoon baking soda
½	teaspoon salt
⅔	cup finely chopped dried apricots
¼	cup plus 2 tablespoons unblanched sliced almonds, divided
1	cup mashed ripe bananas (about 2 medium bananas)
½	cup low-fat buttermilk
⅓	cup vegetable oil
⅓	cup packed light brown sugar
2	eggs
¼	teaspoon almond extract

1. Heat oven to 350°F. Spray bottom only of 9×5-inch loaf pan with nonstick cooking spray. Coat bottom of pan with flour; tap out excess.

2. Combine flour, oats, baking powder, baking soda and salt in large bowl; mix well. Add apricots and ¼ cup almonds; mix well.

3. Whisk together bananas, buttermilk, oil, brown sugar, eggs and extract in medium bowl until well blended. Add to dry ingredients all at once; stir just until dry ingredients are evenly moistened. (Do not overmix.) Pour into pan. Sprinkle with remaining 2 tablespoons almonds.

4. Bake 55 to 65 minutes or until golden brown and wooden pick inserted in center comes out clean. Cover 10 minutes in pan on wire rack. Remove bread from pan. Cool completely on rack.

Makes 1 loaf

Note: To store, wrap covered bread tightly in aluminum foil and store up to 3 days at room temperature. For longer storage, label and freeze.

Nutrition Information (½ of 1-inch slice): *Calories 170 (calories from fat 50), total fat 6g, saturated fat 1g, cholesterol 25mg, sodium 190mg, carbohydrates 25g, dietary fiber 2g, protein 4g*

Blueberry-Ginger Muffin Tops

1½ **cups Quaker® Oats (quick or old fashioned, uncooked)**
½   **cup granulated sugar**
⅓   **cup (5 tablespoons plus 1 teaspoon) margarine or butter, melted, divided**
1⅓ **cups all-purpose flour**
1   **tablespoon baking powder**
¾   **teaspoon ground ginger**
⅔   **cup milk**
1   **egg, lightly beaten**
1   **cup blueberries, fresh or frozen**

1. Heat oven to 400°F. Lightly grease large cookie sheet.

2. Combine oats and sugar in large bowl; mix well. For streusel topping, combine ¼ cup oat mixture and 1 tablespoon melted margarine in small bowl. Set aside.

3. For muffins, add flour, baking powder and ginger to remaining oat mixture; mix well. Combine milk, remaining melted margarine and egg in small bowl; mix well. Add to dry ingredients; mix just until dry ingredients are moistened. Stir in blueberries. For each muffin top, drop batter by ¼ cupfuls onto prepared cookie sheet. Sprinkle streusel topping evenly over batter, patting gently.

4. Bake 20 to 22 minutes or until golden brown. Serve warm.

Makes 12 muffins

Note: To freeze, wrap muffin tops securely in foil, or place in freezer bag; label and freeze. To reheat, microwave at HIGH (100% power) about 30 seconds per muffin top.

Nutrition Information (1 muffin top): Calories 190 (calories from fat 63), total fat 7g, saturated fat 1g, cholesterol 20mg, sodium 190mg, carbohydrates 29g, dietary fiber 2g, protein 4g

North Country Rosemary-Olive Scones

1½   cups all-purpose flour
 1   cup Quaker® Oats (quick or old fashioned, uncooked)
 1   tablespoon granulated sugar
 2   teaspoons baking powder
1½   teaspoons chopped fresh rosemary or ½ teaspoon dried
       rosemary, crushed
 ¾   teaspoon black pepper
 ½   teaspoon salt (optional)
 ½   cup (1 stick) butter or margarine, chilled
 ⅓   cup half-and-half or milk
 2   eggs, lightly beaten
 ⅓   cup finely chopped onion
 ¼   cup kalamata or ripe olives, pitted and coarsely chopped

1. Heat oven to 425°F. Lightly grease cookie sheet.

2. Combine flour, oats, sugar, baking powder, rosemary, pepper and, if desired, salt in large bowl. Cut in butter with pastry blender or 2 knives until mixture resembles coarse crumbs.

3. Combine remaining ingredients in medium bowl; mix well. Add to dry ingredients; mix just until dry ingredients are moistened. Turn out onto lightly floured surface; knead 8 to 10 times. Pat dough into 8-inch circle about ¾ inch thick. Cut into 8 wedges; place wedges on cookie sheet.

4. Bake 18 to 20 minutes or until light golden brown. Serve warm.

Makes 8 scones

Nutrition Information (1 scone): Calories 240 (calories from fat 120), total fat 13g, saturated fat 3g, cholesterol 0mg, sodium 280mg, carbohydrates 26g, dietary fiber 2g, protein 6g

Quaker's Best Oatmeal Muffins

Streusel

⅓ cup Quaker® Oats (quick or old fashioned, uncooked)
¼ cup all-purpose flour
¼ cup packed brown sugar
3 tablespoons margarine or butter, chilled and cut into pieces

Muffins

1½ cups all-purpose flour
1 cup Quaker® Oats (quick or old fashioned, uncooked)
½ cup granulated sugar
1 tablespoon baking powder
1 cup low-fat (2%) milk
¼ cup vegetable oil
1 egg, lightly beaten
1 teaspoon vanilla

1. Heat oven to 400°F. Line 12 medium muffin cups with paper baking cups or spray bottoms only with nonstick cooking spray.

2. For streusel, combine oats, flour and brown sugar in small bowl; mix well. Cut in margarine with pastry blender or 2 knives until mixture is crumbly. Set aside.

3. For muffins, combine flour, oats, granulated sugar and baking powder in large bowl; mix well. Combine milk, oil, egg and vanilla in small bowl; mix well. Add to dry ingredients all at once; stir just until dry ingredients are moistened. (Do not overmix.) Fill muffin cups almost full. Sprinkle with reserved streusel, patting gently.

4. Bake 18 to 20 minutes or until golden brown. Cool muffins in pan on wire rack 5 minutes. Remove from pan. Serve warm.

Makes 12 muffins

Nutrition Information (1 muffin): *Calories 240 (calories from fat 80), total fat 9g, saturated fat 2g, cholesterol 20mg, sodium 170mg, carbohydrates 34g, dietary fiber 1g, protein 5g*

Fruited Oat Scones

1½	**cups all-purpose flour**
1¼	**cups Quaker® Oats (quick or old fashioned, uncooked)**
¼	**cup granulated sugar**
1	**tablespoon baking powder**
¼	**teaspoon salt (optional)**
⅓	**cup (5 tablespoons plus 1 teaspoon) margarine or butter**
1⅓	**cups (6-ounce package) diced dried mixed fruit**
½	**cup milk**
1	**egg, lightly beaten**
1	**teaspoon granulated sugar**
⅛	**teaspoon ground cinnamon**

1. Heat oven to 375°F. Lightly grease cookie sheet.

2. Combine flour, oats, ¼ cup sugar, baking powder and, if desired, salt in large bowl. Cut in margarine with pastry blender or 2 knives until mixture resembles coarse crumbs; stir in fruit. Add milk and egg, mixing just until dry ingredients are moistened. Shape dough into ball.

3. Turn out onto lightly floured surface; knead gently 6 times. Pat dough into 8-inch circle about ¾ inch thick on cookie sheet. Score round into 12 wedges with sharp knife. Combine 1 teaspoon sugar and cinnamon; sprinkle over dough.

4. Bake 28 to 30 minutes or until light golden brown. Break apart; serve warm.

Makes 12 scones

Nutrition Information (1 scone):
Calories 195 (calories from fat 55), total fat 6g, saturated fat 1g, cholesterol 18mg, sodium 193mg, carbohydrates 32g, dietary fiber 2g, protein 4g

Italian Herbed Oatmeal Focaccia

2 tablespoons cornmeal
1½ to 2¼ cups all-purpose flour, divided
1 cup Quaker® Oats (quick or old fashioned, uncooked)
2 tablespoons dried Italian seasoning, divided
1 package (¼ ounce) quick-rising active dry yeast (2¼ teaspoons)
2 teaspoons granulated sugar
1½ teaspoons garlic salt, divided
1 cup water
¼ cup plus 2 tablespoons olive oil, divided
4 to 6 sun-dried tomatoes packed in oil, drained and chopped
¼ cup grated Parmesan cheese

1. Lightly spray 13 × 9-inch baking pan with nonstick cooking spray; dust with cornmeal. In large bowl, combine 1 cup flour, oats, 1 tablespoon Italian seasoning, yeast, sugar and 1 teaspoon garlic salt; mix well.

2. In small saucepan, heat water and ¼ cup oil until very warm (120° to 130°F); stir into flour mixture. Gradually stir in enough remaining flour to make a soft dough. Turn dough out onto lightly floured surface. Knead 8 to 10 minutes or until smooth and elastic. Cover and let rest 10 minutes.

3. Pat dough into prepared pan, pressing dough out to edges of pan. Using fingertips, poke indentations over surface of dough. Brush remaining 2 tablespoons oil over dough. Sprinkle with remaining 1 tablespoon Italian seasoning and ½ teaspoon garlic salt. Arrange tomatoes across top; sprinkle with cheese. Cover; let rise in warm place until doubled, about 30 minutes.

4. Heat oven to 400°F. Bake 25 to 30 minutes or until golden brown. Cut into strips or squares. Serve warm.

Makes 12 servings

Nutrition Information (1 focaccia strip [¹⁄₁₂ of loaf]): Calories 170 (calories from fat 70), total fat 8g, saturated fat 1g, cholesterol 1mg, sodium 190mg, carbohydrates 19g, dietary fiber 1g, protein 4g

Lemon Poppy Seed Oatmeal Muffins

Streusel

¼	cup Quaker® Oats (quick or old fashioned, uncooked)
1	tablespoon granulated sugar
1	tablespoon margarine or butter, melted

Muffins

1½	cups all-purpose flour
1	cup Quaker® Oats (quick or old fashioned, uncooked)
⅔	cup granulated sugar
4	teaspoons poppy seeds
2	teaspoons baking powder
½	teaspoon baking soda
¾	cup low-fat (2%) or fat-free (skim) milk
¼	cup vegetable oil
2	egg whites or 1 egg, lightly beaten
1	tablespoon lemon juice
2	teaspoons grated lemon peel

1. Heat oven to 400°F. Line 12 medium muffin cups with paper baking cups or spray bottoms only with nonstick cooking spray.

2. For streusel, combine oats, sugar and margarine in small bowl; mix well. Set aside.

3. For muffins, combine flour, oats, sugar, poppy seeds, baking powder and baking soda; mix well. Combine milk, oil, egg whites, lemon juice and lemon peel in small bowl; mix well. Add to dry ingredients all at once; mix just until dry ingredients are moistened. Fill muffin cups almost full. Sprinkle with reserved streusel, patting gently.

4. Bake 18 to 20 minutes or until light golden brown. Cool muffins in pan on wire rack 5 minutes. Remove from pan. Cool completely.

Makes 12 muffins

Note: To freeze, place individual muffins in small freezer bag; freeze. Thaw at room temperature, or unwrap and microwave on HIGH about 30 seconds per muffin.

Nutrition Information (1 muffin): Calories 200 (calories from fat 60) total fat 7g, saturated fat 1g, cholesterol 0mg, sodium 140mg, carbohydrates 31g, dietary fiber 1g, protein 4g

Pineapple-Macadamia Oatmeal

1 **can (20 ounces) pineapple tidbits in pineapple juice
Water**

¼ **teaspoon salt**

2 **cups Quaker® Oats (quick or old fashioned, uncooked)**

2 **containers (6 ounces each) vanilla fat-free yogurt***

¼ **to ½ teaspoon ground ginger**

⅓ **cup packed brown sugar***

¼ **cup coarsely chopped macadamia nuts or almonds**

*If artificially sweetened yogurt is used, reduce brown sugar to ¼ cup.

1. Drain pineapple tidbits, reserving juice. Set fruit aside. Add enough water to juice to equal 3¼ cups. Bring combined juice and water and salt to a boil in medium saucepan. Stir in oats.

2. Return to a boil; reduce heat to medium. Cook 1 minute for quick oats, 5 minutes for old fashioned oats, or until most of liquid is absorbed, stirring occasionally. Stir in reserved pineapple. Let stand, covered, until desired consistency.

3. Spoon yogurt into small bowl. Add ginger; mix well. Spoon oatmeal into 5 cereal bowls. Top each serving with brown sugar, nuts and yogurt, dividing evenly.

Makes 5 servings

Nutrition Information (1 cup): *Calories 340 (calories from fat 70), total fat 7g, saturated fat 1g, cholesterol 0mg, sodium 130mg, carbohydrates 65g, dietary fiber 5g, protein 8g*

Whole Grain Banana Fruit 'n' Nut Bars

1¼   **cups whole wheat flour**
2   **teaspoons pumpkin pie spice**
½   **teaspoon baking soda**
¼   **teaspoon salt**
⅔   **cup packed brown sugar**
½   **cup (1 stick) light butter**
1   **large egg**
1¼   **cups mashed ripe bananas (about 3 small bananas)**
1½   **cups Quaker® Oats (quick or old fashioned, uncooked)**
⅔   **cup chopped pitted dates or golden raisins**
⅔   **cup chopped toasted walnuts**

1. Heat oven to 350°F. Lightly spray 13 × 9-inch metal baking pan with nonstick cooking spray. Stir together flour, pumpkin pie spice, baking soda and salt in medium bowl; mix well. Set aside.

2. Beat brown sugar and butter in large bowl with electric mixer until well blended. Add egg and bananas; mix well. (Mixture will look curdled.) Add flour mixture; beat on low just until well blended. Stir in oats, dates and walnuts. Spread evenly in prepared pan.

3. Bake 20 to 25 minutes or until edges are golden brown and wooden pick inserted in center comes out with a few moist crumbs clinging to it. Cool completely in pan on wire rack. Cut into bars. To store, wrap tightly in foil and store up to 2 days at room temperature. For longer storage, label and freeze in airtight container up to 3 months. Defrost, uncovered, at room temperature.

Makes 24 bars

Nutrition Information (1 bar): *Calories 130 (calories from fat 45), total fat 4.5g, saturated fat 1.5g, cholesterol 15mg, sodium 90mg, carbohydrates 21g, dietary fiber 2g, protein 3g*

Baked Cherry-Almond Oatmeal

2¼   cups Quaker® Oats (quick or old fashioned, uncooked)
½   cup packed brown sugar
½   teaspoon salt
3   cups low-fat (2%) milk
3   eggs, lightly beaten
1   tablespoon melted butter (optional)
1   teaspoon vanilla
¼   to ½ teaspoon almond extract
¾   cup dried cherries
½   cup toasted sliced almonds
Vanilla low-fat yogurt

1. Heat oven to 350°F. Spray 8 (6-ounce) custard cups or ramekins with nonstick cooking spray; arrange on rimmed baking sheet.

2. Combine oats, brown sugar and salt in large bowl; mix well. Whisk together milk, eggs, butter, if desired, vanilla and almond extract in medium bowl. Add to dry ingredients; mix until well blended. Spoon into cups. Stir cherries into each cup, dividing evenly; sprinkle evenly with almonds.

3. Bake until knife inserted near center comes out clean, about 23 to 26 minutes for quick oats, 25 to 30 minutes for old fashioned oats. (Centers will not be completely set.) Cool 10 minutes. To serve, top with yogurt.

Makes 8 servings

Variations:

• Substitute dried cranberries, blueberries or chopped dried apricots for dried cherries.

• To bake in 8-inch square baking pan, spray pan with nonstick cooking spray. Prepare oatmeal as directed. Pour into pan, stir in cherries and sprinkle with almonds. Bake until knife inserted near center comes out clean, about 30 to 35 minutes.

Nutrition Information (⅛ of recipe): Calories 280 (calories from fat 80), total fat 9g, saturated fat 2.5g, cholesterol 85mg, sodium 220mg, carbohydrates 41g, dietary fiber 3g, protein 11g

Banana Bread Oatmeal

  3   cups fat-free (skim) milk
  3   tablespoons packed brown sugar
  ¾ teaspoon ground cinnamon
  ¼ teaspoon ground nutmeg
  ¼ teaspoon salt (optional)
  2   cups Quaker® Oats (quick or old fashioned, uncooked)
  2   medium-size ripe bananas, mashed (about 1 cup)
  2   to 3 tablespoons coarsely chopped toasted pecans
      Vanilla fat-free yogurt (optional)
      Banana slices (optional)
      Pecan halves (optional)

1. Bring milk, brown sugar, spices and, if desired, salt to a gentle boil in medium saucepan (watch carefully). Stir in oats. Return to a boil; reduce heat to medium. Cook 1 minute for quick oats, 5 minutes for old fashioned oats, or until most of liquid is absorbed, stirring occasionally.

2. Remove oatmeal from heat. Stir in mashed bananas and pecans. Spoon oatmeal into 4 cereal bowls. Top with yogurt, sliced bananas and pecan halves, if desired.

Makes 4 servings

Nutrition Information (¼ of recipe): *Calories 340 (calories from fat 50), total fat 6g, saturated fat 1g, cholesterol <5mg, sodium 100mg, carbohydrates 60g, dietary fiber 6g, protein 14g*

Oaty Pear 'n' Pecan Pancakes

1   **cup Aunt Jemima® Original Pancake Mix**
1   **teaspoon ground cinnamon**
1   **cup milk**
1   **egg**
1   **tablespoon vegetable oil**
1   **medium-firm ripe pear, cored and chopped (about 1 cup)**
¾   **cup Quaker® Oats (quick or old fashioned, uncooked)**
2   **tablespoons chopped toasted pecans**
½   **to ¾ cup Aunt Jemima Lite® Syrup, warmed**
    Pear slices (optional)
    Chopped toasted pecans (optional)

1. Stir together pancake mix and cinnamon in large bowl. Combine milk, egg and oil in medium bowl; mix well. Add to pancake mix; stir with wire whisk just until combined. Gently stir in pear, oats and 2 tablespoons pecans. Let stand 1 to 2 minutes to thicken.

2. Cook pancakes on hot griddle according to package directions. Serve with syrup and, if desired, pear slices and additional pecans.

Makes 12 pancakes

Cook's tip: To toast nuts, spread in single layer on cookie sheet. Bake at 350°F 6 to 8 minutes or until lightly browned and fragrant, stirring occasionally. Cool before using. Or spread in single layer on microwave-safe plate. Microwave on HIGH (100% power) 1 minute; stir. Continue to microwave on HIGH, checking every 30 seconds, until nuts are fragrant and brown. Cool before using.

Nutrition Information (3 pancakes): Calories 360 (calories from fat 90), total fat 10g, saturated fat 2g, cholesterol 60mg, sodium 690mg, carbohydrates 58g, dietary fiber 4g, protein 10g

Berry-Almond Crumble Oatmeal

Topping

½	cup Quaker® Oats (quick or old fashioned, uncooked)
¼	cup sliced almonds
⅓	cup packed brown sugar
½	teaspoon ground cinnamon

Oatmeal

3	cups fat-free (skim) milk or low-fat soy drink
1½	teaspoons ground cinnamon
¼	teaspoon salt (optional)
2	cups Quaker® Oats (quick or old fashioned, uncooked)
1	cup blueberries, frozen (do not thaw) or canned (drained)

1. For topping, combine oats and almonds in medium skillet. Cook over medium-low heat 4 to 6 minutes, stirring occasionally, until both are lightly browned. Cool completely. Combine brown sugar and cinnamon in small bowl. Add oat mixture; mix well.

2. For oatmeal, bring milk, cinnamon and, if desired, salt to a boil in medium saucepan; stir in oats. Return to a boil; reduce heat to medium. Cook 1 minute for quick oats or 5 minutes for old fashioned oats, stirring occasionally. Gently stir in blueberries. Continue cooking, until blueberries are heated through and most of liquid is absorbed, about 1 minute. Spoon oatmeal into 5 cereal bowls. Sprinkle topping over oatmeal.

Makes 5 servings

Nutrition Information (⅕ of recipe): *Calories 370 (calories from fat 60), total fat 7g, saturated fat 0g, cholesterol <5mg, sodium 90mg, carbohydrates 68g, dietary fiber 6g, protein 13g*

Orange-Banana-Date Oatmeal

2 **cups orange juice**
1 **cup water**
¼ **teaspoon salt (optional)**
⅛ **teaspoon ground nutmeg**
1½ **cups Quaker® Oats (quick or old fashioned, uncooked)**
¾ **cup chopped dates or raisins**
1 **medium-size ripe banana, mashed**

1. In medium saucepan, bring juice, water, salt, if desired, and nutmeg to a boil. Stir in oats and dates.

2. Return to a boil; reduce heat to medium. Cook 1 minute for quick oats, 5 minutes for old fashioned oats, or until most of liquid is absorbed, stirring occasionally. Stir in banana. Let stand until desired consistency.

Makes 4 servings

Microwave Directions: Combine all ingredients except banana in 3-quart microwave-safe bowl. Microwave on HIGH (100% power) 6 to 7 minutes for quick oats, 9 to 10 minutes for old fashioned oats, or until most of the liquid is absorbed. Stir in banana. Let stand until desired consistency.

Nutrition Information (¼ of recipe): *Calories 290 (calories from fat 20), total fat 2g, saturated fat 0g, cholesterol 0mg, sodium 5mg, carbohydrates 25g, dietary fiber 6g, protein 7g*

Maple-Apple Oatmeal

3   **cups apple juice**
½   **teaspoon ground cinnamon**
¼   **teaspoon salt (optional)**
1½   **cups Quaker® Oats (quick or old fashioned, uncooked)**
½   **cup chopped fresh or dried apple**
¼   **cup Aunt Jemima® Original Syrup**
½   **cup chopped nuts (optional)**

1. Bring juice, cinnamon and, if desired, salt to a boil in medium saucepan. Stir in oats, apple and syrup.

2. Return to a boil; reduce heat to medium. Cook 1 minute for quick oats, 5 minutes for old fashioned oats, or until most of juice is absorbed, stirring occasionally. Stir in nuts, if desired. Let stand until desired consistency.

Makes 4 servings

Microwave Directions: Combine all ingredients, except nuts, in 3-quart microwave-safe bowl. Microwave on HIGH (100% power) 6 to 7 minutes for quick oats, 9 to 10 minutes for old fashioned oats, or until most of juice is absorbed. Stir in nuts, if desired. Let stand until desired consistency.

Nutrition Information (¼ of recipe): Calories 260 (calories from fat 20), total fat 2g, saturated fat 0g, cholesterol 0mg, sodium 30mg, carbohydrates 55g, dietary fiber 4g, protein 5g

MAIN DISHES

ABC Meatball Soup

Meatballs

1	pound ground turkey breast or lean ground beef
¾	cup Quaker® Oats (quick or old fashioned, uncooked)
⅓	cup barbecue sauce or ketchup

Soup

1	can (49 ounces) reduced-sodium, fat-free chicken broth
¼	cup alphabet-shaped pasta
1	package (10 ounces) frozen mixed vegetables (do not thaw)

1. Heat broiler. Lightly spray rack of broiler pan with nonstick cooking spray.

2. Combine turkey, oats and barbecue sauce in large bowl; mix lightly but thoroughly. Transfer mixture to sheet of foil. Pat into 9 × 6-inch rectangle. Cut into 1½-inch squares; roll each square into ball. Arrange meatballs on broiler pan.

3. Broil meatballs 6 to 8 inches from heat 6 minutes or until cooked through, turning once.

4. While meatballs cook, bring chicken broth to a boil in 4-quart saucepan or Dutch oven over medium-high heat. Add pasta and frozen vegetables; return to a boil. Reduce heat; cover and simmer 8 minutes or until vegetables and pasta are tender. Add meatballs and cook 1 minute. Serve immediately.

Makes 6 servings

Cook's Tip: Garlic powder, onion powder or dried thyme may be added to the meatball ingredients.

Nutrition Information (⅙ of recipe): Calories 200 (calories from fat 30), total fat 3g, saturated fat <1g, cholesterol 35mg, sodium 720mg, carbohydrates 19g, dietary fiber 4g, protein 25g

Spicy Oat-Crusted Chicken with Sunshine Salsa

Sunshine Salsa
- ¾ cup prepared salsa
- ¾ cup coarsely chopped orange sections

Chicken
- 2 tablespoons canola oil
- 1 tablespoon margarine, melted
- 2 teaspoons chili powder
- 1 teaspoon garlic powder
- 1 teaspoon ground cumin
- ¾ teaspoon salt
- 1½ cups Quick Quaker® Oats, uncooked
- 1 egg, lightly beaten
- 1 tablespoon water
- 4 boneless, skinless chicken breast halves (about 5 to 6 ounces each)
- Chopped fresh cilantro (optional)

1. Combine salsa and orange sections in small bowl. Refrigerate, covered, until serving time.

2. Heat oven to 375°F. Line baking sheet with aluminum foil. Stir together oil, margarine, chili powder, garlic powder, cumin and salt in flat, shallow dish. Add oats, stirring until evenly moistened.

3. Beat egg and water with fork until frothy in second flat, shallow dish. Dip chicken into egg mixture, then coat completely in seasoned oats. Place chicken on foil-lined baking sheet. Pat any extra oat mixture onto top of chicken.

4. Bake 30 minutes or until chicken is cooked through and oat coating is golden brown. Serve with salsa. Garnish with cilantro, if desired.

Makes 4 servings

Nutrition Information (¼ of recipe): Calories 440 (calories from fat 150), total fat 17g, saturated fat 2.5g, cholesterol 150mg, sodium 870mg, carbohydrates 30g, dietary fiber 5g, protein 45g

Mu Shu Meatball Wraps

Meatballs
- 1   **pound lean ground turkey or lean ground beef**
- ¾   **cup Quaker® Oats (quick or old fashioned, uncooked)**
- ½   **cup finely chopped water chestnuts**
- ⅓   **cup chopped green onions**
- 1   **clove garlic, minced**
- 1   **teaspoon finely chopped fresh ginger or ¼ teaspoon ground ginger**
- ¼   **cup light soy sauce**
- 1   **tablespoon water**

Wraps
- ¾   **cup prepared plum sauce**
- 6   **(10-inch) flour tortillas, warmed**
- 1½   **cups coleslaw mix or combination of shredded cabbage and shredded carrots**

1. Heat oven to 350°F. Combine all meatball ingredients in large bowl; mix lightly but thoroughly. Shape into 24 (1½-inch) meatballs; arrange on rack of broiler pan.

2. Bake 20 to 25 minutes or until centers are no longer pink (170°F for turkey; 160°F for beef).

3. To prepare wraps, spread plum sauce on flour tortilla; add about ¼ cup coleslaw mix and 4 hot meatballs. Fold sides of tortilla to center, overlapping edges; fold bottom and top of tortilla under, completely enclosing filling. Repeat with remaining ingredients. Cut wrap in half to serve.

Makes 6 servings

Nutrition Information (⅙ of recipe): *Calories 430 (calories from fat 90), total fat 10g, saturated fat 2.5g, cholesterol 50mg, sodium 760mg, carbohydrates 60g, dietary fiber 5g, protein 24g*

Three Pepper Oat Pilaf

½   **cup chopped red bell pepper**
½   **cup chopped yellow bell pepper**
½   **cup chopped mushrooms**
½   **cup sliced green onions**
2   **garlic cloves, minced**
1   **tablespoon canola or olive oil**
1¾ **cups Old Fashioned Quaker® Oats, uncooked**
2   **egg whites or 1 egg, lightly beaten**
¾   **cup low-fat chicken broth**
2   **tablespoons minced fresh basil or 2 teaspoons dried basil**
½   **teaspoon salt**
¼   **teaspoon black pepper**

1. Cook peppers, mushrooms, green onions and garlic in oil in 10-inch nonstick skillet over medium heat, stirring occasionally, until vegetables are crisp-tender, about 2 minutes.

2. Mix oats and egg whites in large bowl until oats are evenly coated. Add oats to vegetable mixture in skillet.

3. Cook over medium heat, stirring occasionally, until oats are dry and separated, about 5 to 6 minutes. Add broth, basil, salt and pepper. Continue cooking, stirring occasionally, 2 to 3 minutes or until liquid is absorbed. Serve immediately.

Makes 6 servings

Nutrition Information (⅙ of recipe): *Calories 130 (calories from fat 36), total fat 4g, saturated fat 0g, cholesterol 0mg, sodium 310mg, carbohydrates 18g, dietary fiber 3g, protein 6g*

Dilled Salmon Cakes

Sauce

- ½ cup plain fat-free yogurt
- ⅓ cup seeded, chopped tomato
- ⅓ cup seeded, chopped cucumber
- 1 tablespoon finely chopped onion
- 1 tablespoon finely chopped fresh dill or 1 teaspoon dried dill weed

Salmon cakes

- 1 can (14¾ ounces) pink salmon, drained, skin and bones removed
- ¾ cup Quaker® Oats (quick or old fashioned, uncooked)
- ⅓ cup fat-free (skim) milk
- 2 egg whites, lightly beaten
- 2 tablespoons finely chopped onion
- 1 tablespoon finely chopped fresh dill or 1 teaspoon dried dill weed
- ¼ teaspoon salt (optional)

1. For sauce, combine yogurt, tomato, cucumber, onion and dill in small bowl; mix well. Cover and chill while making salmon cakes.

2. For salmon cakes, combine salmon, oats, milk, egg whites, onion, dill and, if desired, salt in medium bowl; mix well. Let stand 5 minutes. Shape into 5 oval patties about 1 inch thick.

3. Lightly spray nonstick skillet with nonstick cooking spray. Cook salmon cakes over medium heat 3 to 4 minutes on each side or until golden brown and heated through. Serve with sauce.

Makes 5 servings

Nutrition Information (⅕ of recipe): *Calories 180 (calories from fat 45), total fat 5g, saturated fat 1.5g, cholesterol 30mg, sodium 110mg, carbohydrates 12g, dietary fiber 2g, protein 21g*

Tex-Mex Meatloaf with Corn Salsa

1   **pound lean ground beef**
1   **cup Quaker® Oats (quick or old fashioned, uncooked)**
1   **jar (16 ounces) picante sauce or salsa, divided**
1   **can (15.25 ounces) whole-kernel corn, drained, divided**
½   **cup chopped onion**
1   **egg, lightly beaten**
2   **tablespoons finely chopped fresh cilantro or parsley, divided (optional)**
1   **teaspoon chili powder**

1. Heat oven to 350°F. For meatloaf, combine ground beef, oats, ¾ cup picante sauce, ½ cup corn, onion, egg, 1 tablespoon cilantro, if desired, and chili powder; mix well. Press into 8 × 4-inch loaf pan or shape into loaf and place in 8 × 8-inch square baking pan.

2. Bake 55 to 60 minutes or until cooked through and no longer pink (160°F). Let stand 5 minutes before serving.

3. For salsa, combine remaining picante sauce, corn and, if desired, cilantro; mix well. Serve with meatloaf.

Makes 8 servings

Nutrition Information (⅛ of recipe): *Calories 250 (calories from fat 100), total fat 11g, saturated fat 4g, cholesterol 65mg, sodium 575mg, carbohydrates 23g, dietary fiber 2g, protein 14g*

Mediterranean Meatloaf

¼   **cup sun-dried tomatoes (about 1 ounce)**
1   **package (10 ounces) frozen chopped spinach, thawed and drained**
½   **cup chopped onion**
¼   **cup crumbled feta cheese**
1½   **pounds lean ground turkey**
1   **cup Quaker® Oats (quick or old fashioned, uncooked)**
1   **teaspoon garlic powder**
1   **teaspoon dried oregano**
½   **teaspoon salt (optional)**
¼   **teaspoon black pepper**
½   **cup fat-free (skim) milk**

1. Heat oven to 400°F. Soften tomatoes according to package directions. Set aside.

2. Cook and stir spinach and onion in small skillet over low heat 4 to 5 minutes or until onion is tender. Remove from heat; cool slightly. Stir in cheese. Set aside.

3. Combine turkey, oats, garlic powder, oregano, salt, if desired, pepper, milk and reserved tomatoes in large bowl; mix lightly but thoroughly. Shape ⅔ of turkey mixture into 9 × 6-inch loaf and place on rack of broiler pan. Make deep indentation down center of loaf, leaving about 1½ inches around edges of loaf. Fill with spinach mixture. Top with remaining turkey mixture. Seal edges to completely enclose filling.

4. Bake 30 to 35 minutes or until meat juices run clear. Let stand 5 minutes before slicing.

Makes 6 servings

Nutrition Information (⅙ of recipe): *Calories 160 (calories from fat 40), total fat 3g, saturated fat 1g, cholesterol 40mg, sodium 1,385mg, carbohydrates 12g, dietary fiber 3g, protein 24g*

DESSERTS

Oatmeal Crème Brûlée

- **2 cups Quick Quaker® Oats or 2¼ cups Old Fashioned Quaker® Oats, uncooked**
- **⅓ cup granulated sugar**
- **¼ teaspoon salt (optional)**
- **3⅓ cups fat-free (skim) milk**
- **½ cup egg substitute or 2 eggs, lightly beaten**
- **2 teaspoons vanilla**
- **⅓ cup packed brown sugar**

1. Heat oven to 350°F. Spray 8-inch square glass baking dish with nonstick cooking spray.

2. Combine oats, granulated sugar and, if desired, salt in large bowl. Combine milk, egg substitute and vanilla in medium bowl; mix well. Add to oat mixture; mix well. Pour into baking dish.

3. Bake 40 to 45 minutes or until center jiggles slightly. Remove from oven to cooling rack.

4. Sprinkle brown sugar evenly over top of oatmeal. Using back of spoon, gently spread sugar into a thin layer across entire surface of oatmeal. Return to oven; bake just until sugar melts, about 2 to 3 minutes. Set oven to broil. Broil 3 inches from heat until sugar bubbles and browns slightly, 1 to 2 minutes. (Watch carefully to prevent burning. It may be necessary to turn baking dish.) Spoon into bowls to serve.

Makes 8 servings

Nutrition Information (⅛ of recipe): Calories 200 (calories from fat 30), total fat 3g, saturated fat 0.5g, cholesterol 55mg, sodium 70mg, carbohydrates 36g, dietary fiber 2g, protein 8g

Caramel-Topped Cheesecakes with Oat-Pecan Crust

1½   **cups Quaker® Oats (quick or old fashioned), uncooked**
½   **cup finely chopped pecans**
1¼   **cups packed light brown sugar, divided**
¼   **cup (½ stick) butter or margarine, melted**
2   **packages (8 ounces each) cream cheese, softened**
1   **teaspoon vanilla**
3   **large eggs, at room temperature**
½   **cup sour cream**
¾   **cup butterscotch caramel topping**
    Sea salt

1. Heat oven to 375°F. Line 18 medium muffin cups with foil liners.

2. Combine oats, pecans, ½ cup brown sugar and butter in large bowl, blending well. Spoon about 2 tablespoons of mixture into bottom of each foil-lined muffin cup, then press evenly and firmly to form crust. Bake 8 to 10 minutes or until golden brown. Remove from oven and cool.

3. Reduce oven temperature to 325°F. Beat cream cheese in large bowl with electric mixer at medium-high speed until light and fluffy, scraping bowl occasionally. Add remaining ¾ cup brown sugar and vanilla; blend well. Add eggs, one at a time, beating just until blended. Add sour cream; mix well. Divide batter evenly among prepared muffin cups. Bake about 20 to 22 minutes or just until set. Cool in pans on wire rack. Chill at least 2 hours.

4. Just before serving, top each individual cheesecake with scant tablespoon of butterscotch caramel topping (if too thick to spread, place in microwave for a few seconds to soften). Sprinkle on a few grains of sea salt and serve.

Makes 18 cheesecakes

GRAND PRIZE WINNER
2006 Quaker® Oats "For Your Heartthrob" Recipe Contest

Nutrition Information (1 cheesecake): *Calories 280 (calories from fat 150), total fat 16g, saturated fat 9g, cholesterol 75mg, sodium 135mg, carbohydrates 31g, dietary fiber <1g, protein 5g*

Mocha Walnut Crunch Coffeecake

Coffeecake

- 1 package (16 ounces) hot roll mix*
- 1 cup Quaker® Oats (quick or old fashioned, uncooked)
- ¼ teaspoon salt (optional)
- ¾ cup milk
- ½ cup (1 stick) margarine or butter
- ½ cup granulated sugar
- 3 eggs, room temperature
- ½ cup semisweet chocolate chips

Topping

- ½ cup all-purpose flour
- ½ cup granulated sugar
- ¼ cup Quaker® Oats (quick or old fashioned, uncooked)
- 1 tablespoon instant coffee granules or espresso powder
- ½ cup (1 stick) margarine or butter, chilled
- ½ cup semisweet chocolate chips
- ½ cup chopped walnuts

Or combine 3 cups all-purpose flour, 2 packets (¼ ounce each) quick-rising active dry yeast (4½ teaspoons) and 1½ teaspoons salt; mix well.

1. Grease 10-inch tube pan or 12-cup Bundt® pan. For coffeecake, combine hot roll mix (including yeast), oats and, if desired, salt in large mixing bowl; mix well.

2. Heat milk and margarine in small saucepan over low heat until margarine is melted; remove from heat. Stir in sugar; cool mixture to 120° to 130°F. Add to oat mixture; add eggs. Beat with electric mixer at low speed until well blended. Stir in ½ cup chocolate chips. Spoon into prepared pan.

3. For topping, combine flour, sugar, oats and coffee granules; cut in margarine with pastry blender or 2 knives until mixture is crumbly. Stir in ½ cup chocolate chips and nuts. Sprinkle evenly over top of dough. Cover loosely with plastic wrap. Let rise in warm place 30 to 40 minutes or until nearly double in size.

4. Heat oven to 350°F. Bake, uncovered, 45 to 50 minutes or until wooden pick inserted near center comes out clean. Cool in pan 10 minutes. Remove from pan, topping side up, onto wire rack. Cool completely. Store tightly covered.

Makes 16 servings

Nutrition Information (¹⁄₁₆ of recipe): *Calories 390 (calories from fat 180), total fat 20g, saturated fat 4.5g, cholesterol 40mg, sodium 370mg, carbohydrates 48g, dietary fiber 4g, protein 7g*

Hidden Berry Cupcakes

1¾ **cups all-purpose flour**
1¼ **cups granulated sugar**
 1   **tablespoon baking powder**
½   **teaspoon salt**
⅓   **cup (5 tablespoons plus 1 teaspoon) butter, softened**
 3   **eggs**
⅔   **cup milk**
 1   **tablespoon vanilla**
 1   **cup Quaker® Oats (quick or old fashioned, uncooked)**
½   **cup seedless strawberry or raspberry fruit spread**
     Confectioners' sugar

1. Heat oven to 350°F. Line 16 medium muffin cups with paper or foil liners. Set aside.

2. Combine flour, sugar, baking powder and salt in large bowl. Add butter and beat with electric mixer on low speed until crumbly, about 1 minute. Combine eggs, milk and vanilla in medium bowl; add to flour mixture. Beat on low speed until incorporated, then on medium speed 2 minutes. Gently fold in oats. Divide batter evenly among muffin cups, filling each about ¾ full.

3. Bake 18 minutes or until a wooden pick inserted in center comes out clean. Remove from pan; cool completely on wire rack.

4. Using small sharp knife, cut cone-shaped piece from center of each cupcake, leaving ¾-inch border around edge of cupcake. Carefully remove and reserve cake pieces. Fill each depression with generous teaspoon of fruit spread. Top with reserved cake pieces; sift confectioners' sugar over tops of cupcakes.

Makes 16 cupcakes

Nutrition Information (1 cupcake): *Calories 210 (calories from fat 50), total fat 5g, saturated fat 3g, cholesterol 50mg, sodium 190mg, carbohydrates 37g, dietary fiber 1g, protein 4g*

Apple Spice Cake

Topping
- 1 cup Quaker® Oats (quick or old fashioned, uncooked)
- ½ cup packed brown sugar
- ½ teaspoon ground cinnamon
- ¼ cup (½ stick) butter, softened
- Whipped cream (optional)

Cake
- 1 package (18.5 ounces) spice cake mix
- 1 cup Quaker® Oats (quick or old fashioned, uncooked)
- 1 cup (8 ounces) plain low-fat yogurt
- 3 eggs
- ¼ cup vegetable oil
- ¼ cup water
- 1½ cups finely chopped apples (about 2 medium)

1. Heat oven to 350°F. Spray 13 × 9-inch metal baking pan with nonstick cooking spray.

2. For topping, combine oats, brown sugar and cinnamon in medium bowl. Cut in butter with pastry blender or 2 knives until mixture is crumbly. Set aside.

3. For cake, combine cake mix, oats, yogurt, eggs, oil and water in large bowl. Blend with electric mixer at low speed until moistened; mix at medium speed 2 minutes. Stir in apples. Pour into pan. Sprinkle topping evenly over batter.

4. Bake 40 to 45 minutes or until wooden pick inserted in center comes out clean. Serve warm or at room temperature with whipped cream, if desired.

Makes 16 servings

Nutrition Information (¹⁄₁₆ of recipe): *Calories 290 (calories from fat 110), total fat 12g, saturated fat 4g, cholesterol 55mg, sodium 270mg, carbohydrates 40g, dietary fiber 1g, protein 6g*

Fudgy Banana Oat Cake

Topping
- 1 **cup Quaker® Oats (quick or old fashioned, uncooked)**
- ½ **cup packed brown sugar**
- ¼ **cup (½ stick) margarine or butter, chilled**

Filling
- 1 **cup (6 ounces) semisweet chocolate chips**
- ⅔ **cup sweetened condensed milk (not evaporated milk)**
- 1 **tablespoon margarine or butter**

Cake
- 1 **package (18.25 ounces) devil's food cake mix**
- 1¼ **cups mashed ripe bananas (about 3 large)**
- ⅓ **cup vegetable oil**
- 3 **eggs**
  Banana slices (optional)
  Sweetened whipped cream (optional)

1. Heat oven to 350°F. Lightly grease bottom only of 13 × 9-inch baking pan or spray with nonstick cooking spray. For topping, combine oats and brown sugar. Cut in margarine with pastry blender or 2 knives until mixture is crumbly. Set aside.

2. For filling, heat chocolate chips, sweetened condensed milk and margarine in small saucepan over low heat until chocolate is melted, stirring occasionally. Remove from heat. Set aside.

3. For cake, combine cake mix, bananas, oil and eggs in large mixing bowl. Blend with electric mixer at low speed until dry ingredients are moistened. Beat at medium speed 2 minutes. Spread batter evenly into prepared pan.

4. Drop chocolate filling by teaspoonfuls evenly over batter. Sprinkle with reserved oat topping. Bake 40 to 45 minutes or until cake pulls away from sides of pan and topping is golden brown. Cool cake in pan on wire rack. Cut into squares. Garnish with banana slices and sweetened whipped cream, if desired.

Makes 15 servings

Nutrition Information (¹⁄₁₅ of recipe): *Calories 400 (calories from fat 170) total fat 18g, saturated fat 5g, cholesterol 45mg, sodium 240mg, carbohydrates 56g, dietary fiber 3g, protein 5g*

Easy Apple-Berry Crumble Pie

1½   **cups Quaker® Oats (quick or old fashioned, uncooked)**
1   **cup all-purpose flour**
½   **cup packed brown sugar**
½   **teaspoon baking soda**
10   **tablespoons butter or margarine, melted**
1   **can (21 ounces) apple pie filling**
¾   **cup dried cranberries**
1½   **teaspoons lemon juice**
½   **teaspoon ground cinnamon**

1. Heat oven to 375°F. Lightly spray 8- or 9-inch glass pie plate with nonstick cooking spray.

2. Combine oats, flour, brown sugar and baking soda in medium bowl. Add melted butter; mix well. Set aside ¾ cup oat mixture for topping. Press remaining oat mixture firmly onto bottom and sides of pie plate. Bake 10 to 12 minutes or until light golden brown. Cool slightly on wire rack.

3. Stir together pie filling, cranberries, lemon juice and cinnamon in same bowl. Spoon filling over hot crust, spreading evenly. Sprinkle reserved oat mixture evenly over filling. Bake 18 to 22 minutes or until topping is golden brown. Serve warm or at room temperature.

Makes 8 servings

Nutrition Information (⅛ of recipe): Calories 400 (calories from fat 140), total fat 16g, saturated fat 9g, cholesterol 40mg, sodium 250mg, carbohydrates 64g, dietary fiber 3g, protein 4g

Not-So-Sinful Sundae Pie

Crust

1 cup Quaker® Oats (quick or old fashioned, uncooked)
½ cup all-purpose flour
5 tablespoons margarine, melted
¼ cup packed brown sugar

Filling

1 quart fat-free or low-fat vanilla frozen yogurt, softened
2 cups any combination of fresh fruit, such as sliced bananas, blueberries or halved strawberries
Fat-free hot fudge topping or berry-flavored fruit syrup (optional)

1. Heat oven to 350°F. Spray 9-inch pie plate with nonstick cooking spray.

2. Combine oats, flour, margarine and brown sugar in medium bowl; mix well. Press firmly onto bottom and sides of pie plate. Bake 18 to 20 minutes or until golden brown. Cool completely on wire rack.

3. Spoon frozen yogurt into cooled crust, spreading evenly. Cover and freeze until firm, about 5 hours. Remove pie from freezer 10 to 15 minutes before serving. Cut into wedges; top with fruit and fudge sauce, if desired. Store tightly covered in freezer.

Makes 8 servings

Nutrition Information (⅛ of recipe): *Calories 280 (calories from fat 80), total fat 9g, saturated fat 1.5g, cholesterol 0mg, sodium 140mg, carbohydrates 43g, dietary fiber 2g, protein 4g*

Autumn Fruit Cobbler

 3 **large apples, cored and cut into ¼-inch wedges**
 2 **medium-firm ripe Bartlett or Bosc pears, peeled, quartered and cored**
 ⅓ **cup dried cranberries**
 1 **cup packed light brown sugar, divided**
 2 **tablespoons cornstarch**
1½ **teaspoons ground cinnamon, divided**
1½ **cups all-purpose flour**
 1 **cup Quaker® Oats (quick or old fashioned, uncooked)**
 2 **teaspoons baking powder**
 ¼ **teaspoon salt**
 ½ **cup (1 stick) margarine or butter, chilled**
 ⅔ **cup low-fat (2%) milk**
   Vanilla ice cream (optional)

1. Heat oven to 400°F. Combine apples, pears and cranberries in large bowl. Combine ¾ cup brown sugar, cornstarch and 1 teaspoon cinnamon in small bowl; mix well. Add to fruit; mix well. Spoon into 2½-quart glass baking dish. Bake, uncovered, 30 minutes.

2. Combine flour, oats, remaining ¼ cup brown sugar, baking powder, salt and remaining ½ teaspoon cinnamon in large bowl; mix well. Cut in margarine with pastry blender or 2 knives until mixture resembles coarse crumbs. Add milk; mix with fork until soft dough forms. Turn out onto lightly floured surface; knead gently 6 to 8 times. Pat dough into ½-inch-thick rectangle. Cut with floured biscuit or cookie cutter.

3. Remove baking dish from oven; stir fruit. Carefully arrange biscuits over hot fruit; press lightly into fruit. Bake 15 to 20 minutes or until biscuits are golden brown and fruit mixture is bubbly. Serve warm with vanilla ice cream, if desired. Cover and refrigerate leftovers.

Makes 8 servings

Nutrition Information (⅛ of recipe): Calories 430 (calories from fat 120), total fat 13g, saturated fat 2.5g, cholesterol 0mg, sodium 310mg, carbohydrates 75g, dietary fiber 5g, protein 5g

COOKIES

Oatmeal Cranberry White Chocolate Chunk Cookies

⅔   cup butter or margarine, softened
⅔   cup packed brown sugar
2   large eggs
1½ cups Quaker® Oats (quick or old fashioned, uncooked)
1½ cups all-purpose flour
1   teaspoon baking soda
½   teaspoon salt
1   package (6 ounces) Ocean Spray® Craisins® Original
     Sweetened Dried Cranberries
⅔   cup white chocolate chunks or chips

1. Preheat oven to 375°F.

2. Beat butter and brown sugar together in medium bowl with electric mixer until light and fluffy. Add eggs; mix well. Combine oats, flour, baking soda and salt in separate bowl. Add to butter mixture in several additions, mixing well after each addition. Stir in sweetened dried cranberries and white chocolate chunks.

3. Drop by rounded teaspoonfuls onto ungreased cookie sheets. Bake 10 to 12 minutes or until golden brown. Cool on wire rack.

Makes 30 cookies

Nutrition Information (1 cookie): *Calories 135 (calories from fat 54), total fat 6g, saturated fat 4g, cholesterol 15mg, sodium 138mg, carbohydrates 18g, dietary fiber 1g, protein 2g*

Oatmeal Chipper Skillet Cookie

½ cup (1 stick) butter, softened
½ cup packed brown sugar
¼ cup granulated sugar
1 egg
1 teaspoon vanilla
¾ cup all-purpose flour
½ teaspoon baking soda
¼ teaspoon salt
1½ cups Quaker® Oats (quick or old fashioned, uncooked)
1 cup semisweet chocolate chips
Vanilla ice cream
Caramel ice cream topping or chocolate syrup (optional)

1. Heat oven to 350°F. Beat butter and sugars in large bowl with electric mixer until creamy. Add egg and vanilla; beat well. Combine flour, baking soda and salt in small bowl; mix well. Add to creamed mixture; mix well. Stir in oats and chocolate chips; mix well.

2. Press dough evenly into bottom of 10-inch nonstick ovenproof skillet.

3. Bake 20 minutes or until top is lightly browned. (Do not overbake; cookie will continue to bake after it is removed from oven.) Cool about 10 minutes. Cut into 8 to 16 wedges. Serve with ice cream and, if desired, caramel topping.

Makes 8 to 16 wedges

Extra-Easy Variation: Gently knead 1 cup *Quaker® Oats* (quick or old fashioned, uncooked) into an 18-ounce package of refrigerated chocolate chip cookie dough. Press evenly into bottom of 10-inch nonstick ovenproof skillet. Bake at 350°F for 20 minutes or until top is lightly browned. Continue as directed above.

Nutrition Information (1 wedge [¹⁄₁₆ of recipe]): Calories 190 (calories from fat 80), total fat 9g, saturated fat 5g, cholesterol 25mg, sodium 140mg, carbohydrates 26g, dietary fiber 2g, protein 3g

Quaker's Best Oatmeal Cookies

1¼ **cups (2½ sticks) margarine or butter, softened**
 ¾ **cup packed brown sugar**
 ½ **cup granulated sugar**
 1 **egg**
 1 **teaspoon vanilla**
1½ **cups all-purpose flour**
 1 **teaspoon baking soda**
 1 **teaspoon ground cinnamon**
 ½ **teaspoon salt (optional)**
 ¼ **teaspoon ground nutmeg**
 3 **cups Quaker® Oats (quick or old fashioned, uncooked)**

1. Heat oven to 375°F. Beat margarine and sugars in large bowl until creamy. Add egg and vanilla; beat well. Combine flour, baking soda, cinnamon, salt, if desired, and nutmeg in medium bowl; mix well. Add to creamed mixture; mix well. Add oats; mix well.

2. Drop dough by rounded tablespoonfuls onto ungreased cookie sheets.

3. Bake 8 to 9 minutes for chewy cookies or 10 to 11 minutes for crisp cookies. Cool 1 minute on cookie sheets. Transfer to wire rack; cool completely. Store tightly covered.

Makes 36 cookies

Bar Cookies: Press dough onto bottom of ungreased 13 × 9-inch baking pan. Bake 25 to 30 minutes or until light golden brown. Cool completely in pan on wire rack. Cut into bars. Store tightly covered. Makes 24 bars.

Variations:

• Omit spices; stir in 1 cup chocolate chips, butterscotch-flavored chips or peanut butter-flavored chips.

• Stir in 1 cup raisins or chopped nuts.

Nutrition Information (1 cookie): Calories 120 (calories from fat 55), total fat 6g, saturated fat 1.5g, cholesterol 0mg, sodium 110mg, carbohydrates 14g, dietary fiber <1g, protein 2g

Choc-Oat-Chip Cookies

1 **cup (2 sticks) margarine or butter, softened**
1 **cup packed brown sugar**
½ **cup granulated sugar**
2 **eggs**
2 **tablespoons milk**
2 **teaspoons vanilla**
1¾ **cups all-purpose flour**
1 **teaspoon baking soda**
½ **teaspoon salt (optional)**
2½ **cups Quaker® Oats (quick or old fashioned, uncooked)**
2 **cups semisweet chocolate chips**
1 **cup coarsely chopped nuts (optional)**

1. Heat oven to 375°F. Beat margarine and sugars in large bowl with electric mixer until creamy. Add eggs, milk and vanilla; beat well. Add flour, baking soda and, if desired, salt; mix well. Stir in oats, chocolate chips and nuts; mix well.

2. Drop by rounded tablespoonfuls onto ungreased cookie sheets.

3. Bake 9 to 10 minutes for a chewy cookie or 12 to 13 minutes for a crisp cookie. Cool 1 minute on cookie sheets; transfer to wire racks. Cool completely. Store in tightly covered container.

Makes 60 cookies

Variations: Prepare cookies as recipe directs, except substitute 1 cup of any of the following for 1 cup chocolate chips: raisins, chopped dried apricots, dried cherries, crushed toffee pieces, candy-coated chocolate pieces or white chocolate baking pieces.

For bar cookies: Press dough evenly into ungreased 13 × 9-inch metal baking pan. Bake 30 to 35 minutes or until light golden brown. Cool completely; cut into bars. Store tightly covered.

Nutrition Information (1 cookie): Calories 100 (calories from fat 45), total fat 5g, saturated fat 1.5g, cholesterol 0mg, sodium 60mg, carbohydrates 12g, dietary fiber 1g, protein 1g

Apple-Oatmeal Spice Cookies

¾	cup packed brown sugar
½	cup granulated sugar
¼	cup (½ stick) margarine, softened
¾	cup apple butter* or applesauce
2	egg whites or 1 egg
2	tablespoons fat-free (skim) milk
2	teaspoons vanilla
1½	cups all-purpose flour
1	teaspoon baking soda
1	teaspoon ground cinnamon
½	teaspoon salt (optional)
¼	teaspoon ground nutmeg (optional)
3	cups Quaker® Oats (quick or old fashioned, uncooked)
1	cup diced dried mixed fruit or raisins

*Look for apple butter in the jam and jelly section of the supermarket.

1. Heat oven to 350°F. Lightly spray cookie sheets with nonstick cooking spray.

2. Beat sugars and margarine in large bowl until well blended. Add apple butter, egg whites, milk and vanilla; beat well. Combine flour, baking soda, cinnamon and, if desired, salt and nutmeg in medium bowl; mix well. Add to creamed mixture; mix well. Stir in oats and dried fruit; mix well. (Dough will be moist.)

3. Drop dough by rounded tablespoonfuls onto cookie sheets.

4. Bake 10 to 12 minutes or until edges are light golden brown. Cool 1 minute on cookie sheets. Transfer to wire rack; cool completely. Store tightly covered.

Makes 32 cookies

Nutrition Information (1 cookie):
Calories 90 (calories from fat 15), total fat 1.5g, saturated fat 0g, cholesterol 0mg, sodium 45mg, carbohydrates 17g, dietary fiber <1g, protein 2g

Double Chocolate Oat Cookies

2   **cups semisweet chocolate chips, divided**
½   **cup (1 stick) butter, softened**
½   **cup granulated sugar**
1   **egg**
¼   **teaspoon vanilla**
¾   **cup all-purpose flour**
¾   **cup Quaker® Oats (quick or old fashioned, uncooked)**
1   **teaspoon baking powder**
¼   **teaspoon baking soda**
¼   **teaspoon salt (optional)**

1. Heat oven to 375°F. Melt 1 cup chocolate chips in small saucepan; set aside. Beat butter and sugar until fluffy. Add melted chocolate, egg and vanilla. Add combined flour, oats, baking powder, baking soda and salt; mix well. Stir in remaining chocolate chips.

2. Drop dough by rounded tablespoonfuls onto ungreased cookie sheets.

3. Bake 8 to 10 minutes or just until set. (Do not overbake. Centers should look soft.) Cool 1 minute on cookie sheets; transfer to wire rack. Cool completely. Store tightly covered.

Makes 36 cookies

Nutrition Information (1 cookie):
Calories 97 (calories from fat 48), total fat 6g, saturated fat 3g, cholesterol 12mg, sodium 43mg, carbohydrates 12g, dietary fiber 1g, protein 1g

Peanut Butter Cup Cookies

1½	**cups packed brown sugar**
1	**cup (2 sticks) margarine or butter, softened**
¾	**cup peanut butter (not reduced-fat)**
2	**eggs**
2	**teaspoons vanilla**
1½	**cups all-purpose flour**
⅓	**cup unsweetened cocoa powder**
1	**teaspoon baking soda**
¼	**teaspoon salt (optional)**
2	**cups Quaker® Oats (quick or old fashioned, uncooked)**
1	**package (9 ounces) miniature peanut butter cup candies, unwrapped, cut into halves or quarters (about 35 candies)**

1. Heat oven to 350°F. Beat brown sugar, margarine and peanut butter until creamy. Add eggs and vanilla; beat well. Combine flour, cocoa powder, baking soda and, if desired, salt in small bowl; mix well. Add to creamed mixture; mix well. Stir in oats and candy; mix well.

2. Drop dough by level ¼ cupfuls 3 inches apart onto ungreased cookie sheets.

3. Bake 12 to 14 minutes or until cookies are slightly firm to the touch. (Do not overbake.) Cool 1 minute on cookie sheets. Transfer to wire rack; cool completely. Store tightly covered.

Makes 36 cookies

Nutrition Information (1 cookie): Calories 190 (calories from fat 100), total fat 11g, saturated fat 3.5g, cholesterol 10mg, sodium 150mg, carbohydrates 21g, dietary fiber 2g, protein 4g

Chocolate-Raspberry Streusel Squares

- 1¼ **cups all-purpose flour**
- 1¼ **cups Quaker® Oats (quick or old fashioned, uncooked)**
- ⅓ **cup granulated sugar**
- ⅓ **cup packed brown sugar**
- ½ **teaspoon baking powder**
- ¼ **teaspoon salt (optional)**
- ¾ **cup (1½ sticks) cold margarine or butter, cut into pieces**
- ¾ **cup raspberry preserves or jam (about 10 ounces)**
- 1 **cup semisweet chocolate chips**
- ¼ **cup chopped almonds (optional)**
- ½ **cup white chips (optional)**

1. Heat oven to 375°F. Combine flour, oats, sugars, baking powder and, if desired, salt in large bowl. Cut in margarine with pastry blender or 2 knives until mixture is crumbly. Reserve 1 cup oat mixture for streusel. Press remaining mixture onto bottom of ungreased 8-inch square baking pan. Bake 10 minutes. Transfer to wire rack.

2. Spread preserves evenly over hot crust to within ½ inch of edges. Sprinkle evenly with chocolate chips. Combine reserved oat mixture and almonds, if desired; sprinkle over chocolate, patting gently.

3. Bake 30 to 35 minutes or until golden brown. Cool completely in pan on wire rack. Drizzle with melted white chips, if desired. Let chocolate set before cutting into squares. Store tightly covered.

Makes 24 squares

Nutrition Information (1 square): *Calories 160 (calories from fat 65), total fat 8g, saturated fat 2.5g, cholesterol 0mg, sodium 70mg, carbohydrates 22g, dietary fiber 1g, protein 2g*

Snow-Covered Almond Crescents

1   cup (2 sticks) margarine or butter, softened
¾   cup powdered sugar
½   teaspoon almond extract or 2 teaspoons vanilla extract
2   cups all-purpose flour
¼   teaspoon salt (optional)
1   cup Quaker® Oats (quick or old fashioned, uncooked)
½   cup finely chopped almonds
    Additional powdered sugar

1. Heat oven to 325°F. Beat margarine, ¾ cup powdered sugar and almond extract in large bowl with electric mixer until light and fluffy. Add flour and, if desired, salt; mix until well blended. Stir in oats and almonds.

2. Shape level measuring tablespoonfuls of dough into crescents. Place on ungreased cookie sheets about 2 inches apart.

3. Bake 14 to 17 minutes or until bottoms are light golden brown. Transfer to wire racks. Sift additional powdered sugar generously over warm cookies. Cool completely. Store tightly covered.

Makes 48 cookies

Nutrition Information (1 cookie):
Calories 70 (calories from fat 40), total fat 4.5g, saturated fat 0.5g, cholesterol 0mg, sodium 45mg, carbohydrates 7g, dietary fiber <1g, protein 1g

Oatmeal Scotchies

1	cup (2 sticks) margarine or butter, softened
¾	cup granulated sugar
¾	cup packed brown sugar
2	eggs
1	teaspoon vanilla
1¼	cups all-purpose flour
1	teaspoon baking soda
½	teaspoon salt (optional)
3	cups Quaker® Oats (quick or old fashioned, uncooked)
2	cups (12 ounces) butterscotch pieces

1. Heat oven to 375°F. Beat margarine and sugars in large bowl until creamy. Add eggs and vanilla; beat well. Combine flour, baking soda and, if desired, salt in small bowl; mix well. Add to creamed mixture; mix well. Add oats and butterscotch pieces; mix well.

2. Drop dough by level tablespoonfuls onto ungreased cookie sheets.

3. Bake 7 to 8 minutes for chewy cookies or 9 to 10 minutes for crisp cookies. Cool 2 minutes on cookie sheets. Transfer to wire rack; cool completely. Store tightly covered.

Makes 48 cookies

Nutrition Information (1 cookie): Calories 120, (calories from fat 55), total fat 6g, saturated fat 2.5g, cholesterol 0mg, sodium 80mg, carbohydrates 15g, dietary fiber 1g, protein 1g

Lemon Yogurt Cookies

½ **cup (1 stick) margarine, softened**
1¼ **cups granulated sugar**
½ **cup plain fat-free yogurt or lemon low-fat yogurt**
2 **egg whites or 1 egg**
1 **tablespoon grated lemon peel**
½ **teaspoon vanilla**
2 **cups Quaker® Oats (quick or old fashioned, uncooked)**
1½ **cups all-purpose flour**
1 **teaspoon baking powder**
½ **teaspoon baking soda**
   Additional granulated sugar
¼ **cup confectioners' sugar**

1. Lightly spray cookie sheets with nonstick cooking spray or oil lightly. Beat margarine and 1¼ cups granulated sugar in large bowl with electric mixer until light and fluffy. Add yogurt, egg whites, lemon peel and vanilla; mix until well blended. Combine oats, flour, baking powder and baking soda in medium bowl; mix well. Gradually add to creamed mixture; mix well. Cover and refrigerate 1 to 3 hours.

2. Heat oven to 375°F. With lightly floured hands, shape dough into 1-inch balls; place on prepared cookie sheets. Using bottom of glass dipped in granulated sugar, press into ⅛-inch-thick circles.

3. Bake 10 to 12 minutes or until edges are lightly browned. Cool 2 minutes on cookie sheets; transfer to wire racks. Sift confectioners' sugar over warm cookies. Cool completely. Store tightly covered.

Makes 48 cookies

Nutrition Information (1 cookie): *Calories 70 (calories from fat 20), total fat 2g, saturated fat 0g, cholesterol 0mg, sodium 45mg, carbohydrates 11g, dietary fiber 0g, protein 1g*

Peanutty Crisscrosses

1½ **cups packed brown sugar**
1 **cup peanut butter**
¾ **cup (1½ sticks) margarine or butter, softened**
⅓ **cup water**
1 **egg**
1 **teaspoon vanilla**
3 **cups Quaker® Oats (quick or old fashioned, uncooked)**
1½ **cups all-purpose flour**
½ **teaspoon baking soda**
Granulated sugar

1. Beat brown sugar, peanut butter and margarine in large bowl with electric mixer until creamy. Add water, egg and vanilla; beat well. Combine oats, flour and baking soda in medium bowl; mix well. Add to creamed mixture; mix well. Cover; chill about 2 hours.

2. Heat oven to 350°F. Shape dough into 1-inch balls. Place 2 inches apart on ungreased cookie sheets; flatten with tines of fork, dipped in granulated sugar, to form crisscross pattern. Bake 9 to 10 minutes or until edges are golden brown. Cool 2 minutes on cookie sheets; transfer to wire racks. Cool completely. Store tightly covered.

Makes 84 cookies

Nutrition Information (1 cookie): *Calories 70 (calories from fat 30), total fat 3.5g, saturated fat 0.5g, cholesterol <5mg, sodium 40mg, carbohydrates 8g, dietary fiber <1g, protein 1g*

Tic-Tac-Toe Treats

1 **package (18 ounces) refrigerated sugar cookie dough**
1 **cup Quaker® Oats (quick or old fashioned, uncooked)**
1 **teaspoon ground cinnamon**
  Assorted decorator icings, small candies or candy sprinkles

1. Heat oven to 350°F. Lightly grease cookie sheets or spray with nonstick spray.

2. Break up cookie dough in large bowl. Add oats and cinnamon; knead dough until well mixed.

3. Press dough into 10 × 14-inch rectangle (about ⅛ inch thick) on cookie sheet. Using pizza cutter or thin-bladed knife, cut rectangle into 2-inch squares. (Do not separate.) Using dull side of table knife, gently press tic-tac-toe grid into each cookie. (Do not cut completely through cookies.)

4. Bake 16 to 18 minutes or until edges are golden and middle is set but soft. Immediately cut into 2-inch squares again, if necessary. Transfer cookies to wire rack; cool completely. (If cookies begin to stick to cookie sheet, return to the oven for 1 to 2 minutes to soften.)

5. Decorate cookies as desired with icings, candies or sprinkles.

Makes 35 cookies

Cook's Tip: If desired, substitute 1 package (18 ounces) refrigerated peanut butter cookie dough for sugar cookie dough.

Nutrition Information (1 cookie): Calories 70 (calories from fat 30), total fat 3g, saturated fat 1g, cholesterol <5mg, sodium 60mg, carbohydrates 10g, dietary fiber 0g, protein 1g

Dinosaur Egg Cookies

1	cup (2 sticks) margarine or butter, softened
1	cup confectioners' sugar
1	egg
1	teaspoon vanilla
1½	cups all-purpose flour
1¼	cups Quaker® Oats (quick or old fashioned, uncooked)
½	cup cornstarch
¼	teaspoon salt (optional)
24	assorted bite-size candies
	Colored sugar or candy sprinkles

1. Heat oven to 325°F. Beat margarine and sugar in large bowl with electric mixer until creamy. Add egg and vanilla; beat well. Combine flour, oats, cornstarch and, if desired, salt in medium bowl; mix well. Add to creamed mixture; mix well.

2. Shape rounded tablespoonfuls of dough into 1½-inch balls. Press candy piece into center of each ball; shape dough around candy so it is completely hidden. Lightly pinch one side of dough to form egg shape. Roll cookies in desired decorations until evenly coated. Place 2 inches apart on ungreased cookie sheets.

3. Bake 16 to 20 minutes or until cookies are set and lightly browned on bottom. Remove to wire rack; cool completely. Store tightly covered.

Makes 24 cookies

Nutrition Information (1 cookie): *Calories 150 (calories from fat 90), total fat 10g, saturated fat 2.5g, cholesterol 10mg, sodium 95mg, carbohydrates 19g, dietary fiber <1g, protein 2g*

Chocolate Cookie Bears

1 **cup granulated sugar**
½ **cup (1 stick) butter, softened (do not substitute)**
1 **cup semisweet chocolate chips, melted**
2 **eggs**
1 **teaspoon vanilla**
2 **cups Quaker® Oats (quick or old fashioned, uncooked)**
1½ **cups all-purpose flour**
1 **teaspoon baking powder**
¼ **teaspoon salt (optional)**
Ready-to-spread frosting
Assorted small candies

1. Beat sugar and butter in large bowl with electric mixer until creamy. Add chocolate, eggs and vanilla; beat well. Combine oats, flour, baking powder and, if desired, salt in medium bowl; mix well. Add to chocolate mixture; mix well. Cover; chill about 2 hours.

2. Heat oven to 350°F. To make bears, shape dough into 1-inch balls for bodies, ½-inch balls for heads and ¼-inch balls for arms, legs and ears. On ungreased cookie sheet, gently press pieces together to form bears, placing 2 inches apart. Flatten bears slightly.

3. Bake 8 to 10 minutes or just until firm to the touch. (Do not overbake.) Cool 2 minutes on cookie sheets. Transfer to wire rack; cool completely.

4. Decorate as desired with frosting and candies. Store tightly covered.

Makes 24 cookies

Cook's Tip: To melt chocolate, place in dry microwave-safe measuring cup or small bowl. Microwave on HIGH (100% power) 1 to 2 minutes, stirring every 30 seconds, until smooth. Or place in top part of double boiler over hot (not boiling) water; stir occasionally until smooth.

Nutrition Information (1 bear, undecorated): Calories 150 (calories from fat 55), total fat 6g, saturated fat 2g, cholesterol 15mg, sodium 60mg, carbohydrates 21g, dietary fiber 1g, protein 3g

Chocolate Chip Dulce de Leche Nachos

1 cup Quaker® Oats (quick or old fashioned, uncooked)
½ cup plus 2 tablespoons all-purpose flour, divided
⅓ cup packed light brown sugar
¾ teaspoon ground cinnamon
6 tablespoons butter, melted
⅓ cup chopped salted roasted almonds
½ cup dulce de leche or caramel sauce
4 (7-inch) flour tortillas
¾ cup semisweet chocolate chips

1. Heat oven to 375°F. Combine oats, ½ cup flour, brown sugar and cinnamon in medium bowl; mix well. Add butter; stir until evenly moistened. Stir in almonds. Set aside.

2. Stir together dulce de leche and remaining 2 tablespoons flour in small bowl until blended. Place tortillas on ungreased baking sheets. Spread each tortilla with dulce de leche mixture to within ½ inch of edge; sprinkle evenly with ½ cup chocolate chips, then oat topping. Sprinkle remaining ¼ cup chocolate chips over tortillas.

3. Bake 12 to 14 minutes, or until oat mixture is golden brown and tortilla is crisp on bottom. Cool at least 5 minutes. Cut each tortilla into 6 wedges. Serve warm or cool.

Makes 8 servings

1st PRIZE WINNER

"Seductive Sweets" category winner 2006 Quaker® Oats "For Your Heartthrob" Recipe Contest

Nutrition Information (3 wedges): *Calories 470 (calories from fat 190), total fat 21g, saturated fat 9g, cholesterol 25mg, sodium 270mg, carbohydrates 65g, dietary fiber 6g, protein 6g*

Sparkling Snowflake Cookies

1   **package (18.25 ounces) white cake mix**
1   **cup (2 sticks) butter or margarine, softened**
1   **egg**
1   **teaspoon vanilla**
2   **cups Quaker® Oats (quick or old fashioned, uncooked)**
    Assorted colored sugars, candy sprinkles, small candies or decorator icings (optional)

1. Heat oven to 350°F. Combine half the dry cake mix, butter, egg and vanilla in large bowl; mix thoroughly with large spoon. Stir in remaining cake mix and oats; mix well.

2. Divide dough in half. On well-floured surface, using a well-floured rolling pin, roll each half no more than ¼ inch thick. Cut dough with 3-inch snowflake or other large holiday cookie cutter. Place about 1 inch apart on ungreased cookie sheets. If cookies will be used as tree ornaments, poke hole at top of each cookie with drinking straw before baking. (Repeat immediately after baking if hole closes.)

3. Bake 6 to 8 minutes or just until set (centers may still be soft). Carefully transfer to wire rack; cool completely. Decorate, if desired.

Makes 30 cookies

Decorating Ideas:

• Sprinkle with colored sugars, candy sprinkles or small candies before baking.

• Sprinkle baked cookies with confectioners' sugar as they cool.

• Frost cooled cookies with homemade or ready-to-spread frosting. Sprinkle with edible glitter or colored sugar.

• Squeeze melted dark or white chocolate, decorator frosting or decorator gel in tubes onto cooled cookies.

Note: Dragées (small silver and gold ball-shaped decorations) are inedible and should only be placed on cookies that will be used for decorations and not eaten.

Nutrition Information (1 cookie, undecorated): Calories 140 (calories from fat 70), total fat 8g, saturated fat 1.5g, cholesterol 0mg, sodium 170mg, carbohydrates 16g, dietary fiber 1g, protein 2g

Sweetheart Cookie Puzzle

1   **cup (2 sticks) margarine or butter, softened**
½   **cup granulated sugar**
1   **teaspoon vanilla**
2   **cups Quaker® Oats (quick or old fashioned, uncooked)**
1¼   **cups all-purpose flour**
    Assorted small candies (optional)

1. Heat oven to 350°F. Lightly grease and flour 2 cookie sheets. Using your finger, trace outline of large heart on each cookie sheet.

2. Beat margarine, sugar and vanilla in large bowl with electric mixer until creamy. Combine oats and flour in medium bowl. Add to creamed mixture; mix well.

3. Divide dough in half. With lightly floured hands, pat each half into large heart shape on cookie sheet. If desired, gently press candies into dough. With knife, cut through each heart to form 8 to 10 random shapes. (Do not separate.)

4. Bake 18 to 20 minutes or until lightly browned. Carefully cut through pieces again to separate. Cool 5 minutes on cookie sheet. Transfer to wire rack; cool completely. Store tightly covered.

Makes 2 (10-inch) hearts

Cook's Tip: Small children should use a butter or table knife to cut the random puzzle shapes.

Nutrition Information (2 pieces, undecorated): *Calories 200 (calories from fat 110), total fat 12g, saturated fat 2g, cholesterol 0mg, sodium 135mg, carbohydrates 21g, dietary fiber 1g, protein 3g*

Choc-Oat-Late Honey "Smash" Snacks

2½   **cups thin pretzel sticks, broken into 1-inch pieces**
2¼   **cups Quaker® Oats (quick or old fashioned, uncooked)**
  1   **cup raisins**
  1   **cup dry-roasted peanuts (optional)**
  1   **package (10 ounces) peanut butter-flavored chips**
  2   **cups semisweet chocolate chips**
¾   **cup honey**

1. Line cookie sheet with aluminum foil. Combine pretzels, oats, raisins and, if desired, peanuts in large bowl; mix well. Combine peanut butter-flavored chips, chocolate chips and honey in large saucepan; heat over low heat, stirring constantly, until chips are melted.

2. Immediately pour over oat mixture, stirring until all dry ingredients are coated with chocolate mixture. Spread and "smash" mixture onto foil-lined cookie sheet, working mixture to edges of sheet (mixture will be ⅜ to ½ inch thick, depending on size of cookie sheet). Place in refrigerator until firm. Break into pieces. Store tightly covered at room temperature.

Makes 48 snacks

Cook's Tip: Substitute 1 package (11 ounces) butterscotch-flavored chips for peanut butter-flavored chips.

Nutrition Information (1 piece [¹⁄₄₈ of recipe]): *Calories 130 (calories from fat 45), total fat 5g, saturated fat 2g, cholesterol 0mg, sodium 30mg, carbohydrates 20g, dietary fiber 1g, protein 2g*

Fudgy Peanut Butter Jiffy Cookies

- **2**   **cups granulated sugar**
- **½**   **cup evaporated milk**
- **½**   **cup (1 stick) margarine or butter**
- **¼**   **cup unsweetened cocoa powder**
- **2½**   **cups Quaker® Oats (quick or old fashioned, uncooked)**
- **½**   **cup peanut butter**
- **½**   **cup raisins or chopped dates**
- **2**   **teaspoons vanilla**

Combine sugar, milk, margarine and cocoa in large saucepan. Bring to a boil over medium heat, stirring frequently. Continue boiling 3 minutes. Remove from heat. Stir in oats, peanut butter, raisins and vanilla; mix well. Quickly drop by tablespoonfuls onto waxed paper-lined cookie sheet. Let stand until set. Store tightly covered.

Makes 36 cookies

Nutrition Information (1 cookie): *Calories 120 (calories from fat 45), total fat 5g, saturated fat 1g, cholesterol 0mg, sodium 50mg, carbohydrates 18g, dietary fiber 1g, protein 2g*

3-Minute No-Bake Cookies

- **2**   **cups granulated sugar**
- **½**   **cup (1 stick) margarine or butter**
- **½**   **cup low-fat (2%) milk**
- **⅓**   **cup unsweetened cocoa powder**
- **3**   **cups Quaker® Oats (quick or old fashioned, uncooked)**

Combine sugar, margarine, milk and cocoa in large saucepan. Bring to a boil over medium heat, stirring frequently. Continue boiling 3 minutes. Remove from heat. Stir in oats; mix well. Quickly drop by tablespoonfuls onto waxed paper-lined cookie sheet. Let stand until set. Store tightly covered.

Makes 36 cookies

Nutrition Information (1 cookie): *Calories 90 (calories from fat 30), total fat 3g, saturated fat 0.5g, cholesterol 0mg, sodium 30mg, carbohydrates 16g, dietary fiber <1g, protein 1g*

Banana Split Sundae Cookies

1	cup (2 sticks) margarine or butter, softened
1	cup firmly packed brown sugar
1½	cups mashed ripe bananas (about 4 medium)
2	eggs
2	teaspoons vanilla
2½	cups QUAKER® Oats (quick or old fashioned, uncooked)
2	cups all-purpose flour
1	teaspoon baking soda
¼	teaspoon salt (optional)
1	cup (6 ounces) semisweet chocolate chips
	Ice cream or frozen yogurt
	Ice cream topping, any flavor

1. Heat oven to 350°F. Beat margarine and brown sugar in large bowl with electric mixer until creamy. Add bananas, eggs and vanilla; beat well. Combine oats, flour, baking soda and, if desired, salt in medium bowl; mix well. Add to creamed mixture; mix well. Stir in chocolate chips; mix well.

2. Drop by ¼ cupfuls onto ungreased cookie sheets about 4 inches apart. Spread dough to 3½-inch diameter.

3. Bake 14 to 16 minutes or until edges are light golden brown. Cool 1 minute on cookie sheets; transfer to wire racks. Cool completely. To serve, top each cookie with scoop of ice cream and ice cream topping.

Makes 24 cookies

Nutrition Information (1 cookie [without ice cream or topping]): *Calories 230 (calories from fat 100), total fat 11g, saturated fat 3g, cholesterol 15mg, sodium 140mg, carbohydrates 30g, dietary fiber 2g, protein 3g*